Standing Tall Through It All

Volume III

WILLIE D. KISER-GOLDEN

ISBN: 978-1-5356-0486-4

THE TREE

The tree has always inspired me because of it natural beauty. It displays many phases and images as it grows in width and depth of life.

The limbs grow out from the tree, developing beautiful leaves of colors that change from green, orange, brown, red, and yellow. Limbs can bend or break, but if it doesn't fall off the tree, it will mend and reconnect as a new power of growth through strength and endurance.

The tree can survive with the roots under or on top of the soil and water. It can be cut or sawed down, but unless the roots are damaged or killed the sprouts from the roots continue to live.

Like the tree, in many aspects, life can be a flow of images that display different colors that symbolize a heart of up and downhill journeys, of happy and sad tears, justice, injustice, rain, and sunshine.

The tree can be used in so many ways to enhance our lives. The wood from some trees can be used to build houses, bridges, schools, stores, terminals, and so much more. As a parable to the tree, we can be a source to our family and associates to build a relationship with love, endurance, and "Stand Tall Through It All."

I was inspired to write poems that are proactive in expressing life challenges. Whether rain or shine we carry our own weather. It makes no difference because I am driven by values, and my values are to promote good quality work, even if the weather is desirable or not. The trees are sometimes confronted with different kinds of weather storms, but they endure the hardship of life. We must keep our spirits high and keep pressing forward and endure the pain as well as the goodness of life.

We can count our blessings; be strong in our hearts; revise and connect a new spirit of ideas, love, and endurance; develop a power of integrity; and "Stand Tall Through It All."

DEDICATION

This book is dedicated to all of my family and friends, who inspired and encouraged me to continue to write what God has instilled in my heart to do. Because a "Winner never stop trying."

ACKNOWLEDGMENTS

My thanks to many friends to name a few. The late Charles P. Jones, who was very instrumental in making sure that all of my I's were dotted and my T's were crossed during the writing of this book.

Rhonda Kennedy Adams, who was there when everyone else was too busy to even listen to the idea of my writing. She was there to assist and support me when I was in doubt about certain situations concerning my writing.

Thanks to the late Sutrene Jackson for her support in keeping me motivated to continue to write. She encouraged me to keep the idea of writing on the front burner and not to put it off until a later date. Also, she kept me inspired with hope to keep fulfilling my dream to write poetry.

Dorothy J. Pryor-Sikes would stop from her busy schedule to listen over the telephone to some of my poems and laugh because she could identify, recognize, and envision some of the quests of life that were illustrated in my poems.

Patricia B. always called to let me know when a well-known contact person was in town for the publicity of my poems.

Kelly C. was like a backup for spelling when my mind for spelling went totally blank.

Dorothy Waver Smith, without hesitation, occasionally favored me with advice on correct sentence structure.

My dear husband, Roosevelt Golden, who patiently supported me in writing and getting these poems printed. He wanted his grandchildren to read about the experiences and facets of life that I had endured while "Standing Tall Through It All."

All of the above names were very inspiring in helping me press forward with my writing and to continue striving to be the best I can be.

PREFACE

Standing Tall Through It All, Volume III is a continuation of
Standing Tall Through It All, Volume I and Volume II. It is a
collection of thoughts incorporating an understanding of
certain Christian principles. I tried to consider the people
and events that may have influenced my perspective over a
period of time. There are qualities relating to identity, belief,
and love in various forms. Along the way I frequently cite a
spiritual approach to the types of challenges one might find
in this sometimes uncertain modern society.

The book is divided into several segments, each focusing on
an experience or idea, beginning with a grouping marked
"Inspirational," "Endurance," "Love," etc. These are poems
that direct a message of thanks, life of a farm girl, and
envision a comparatively different environment of city and
farm life, and much more for your enjoyment.

Overall, the contribution is designed to communicate facets
of my own process of life, as well as to enlighten and inspire
the reader who may be following a similar course.

I would like to be a good writer someday. It is not necessary
for me to be the best writer, but I want to be a writer who can
put my thoughts on paper such that generations of readers

will understand my scrambled thoughts and absorb the substance of "Standing Tall Through It All."

These poems were written in hopes that they will deliver a message about how blessings will come from God if you accept Him and have faith. There is no limit on the spirit of God working in your life. He has granted me with new visions and truth and has inspired a spirit of joy and gladness. He is motivating me with a cup of strength to aspire other souls who have doubt about the work of God.

The astonishment isn't until you read each poem in each section. You will find some phases of life that you can identify with your life endeavors. These life endeavors may include hardship; the best is yet to come. Tough times don't last, but tough people do. My grandmother used to often say, "If you travel a path without obstacles, it probably doesn't lead anywhere." It is then when you will grasp the full understanding of "Standing Tall Through It All."

ABOUT THE AUTHOR

Willie D. Kiser-Golden was born in Union Springs, Alabama. Her grandparents reared her and four other cousins. Willie is the first born of fourteen siblings to Annie L. Kiser-Wadley of St. Louis, Missouri. She is also the first born of eight siblings to John Ellis, Jr., her father of Union Springs, Alabama.

She graduated from Carver High School in Union Springs, Alabama. She attended Wilberforce University in Ohio. She also attended Davenport University and graduated from Spring Arbor University in Detroit, Michigan.

She is a committed and loyal member of the Wilberforce University Alumni Association, Detroit Chapter. Willie is a philanthropist at heart and has the highest respect for education and freedom for everyone.

INTRODUCTION

This book of poetry is meant to convey a message to elicit my fullest insight of my own true nature and purpose of life. It is my conviction to inspire and mandate a true conscious of myself. When writing these poems this can only be done through honesty, love, prayer, and a connection with God. He can stimulate and guide you to seek the trail of a fulfilling passage in life. And "Stand Tall Through It All."

I want to be a service to humanity. Hopefully, this book will become beneficial to all ethnic groups and contribute peace, love, compassion, kindness, and usefulness as you progress through life's journey. I want to share some of my experiences to let others know that it maybe raining today, but the sun will shine tomorrow. I am a living witness that good things come to a person who has a true heart to do the right things in the eyesight of God. I kept the faith, "kept the drive" and "held on to the rope of hope" while keeping it real with my true self-identity.

This book is divided into several segments. Each segment focuses on experiences, ideas, and visions that are designed to communicate facets of my life, as well as to enlighten and inspire readers who may have had similar experiences in life.

In addition, these attributes are deemed to flourish for a better character of a person considering the circumstances throughout life. I truly hope these poems will represent an effective measure of my worth that will benefit other people—young, old, black, white, red, yellow, and brown. It is a part of my worth to have a kind heart, kind deeds, kind thoughts, and kind words that will help to "Stand Tall Through It All." I shall continue to hold, think, believe and have an opinion on the greater beautiful things in life.

Before these poems were written, my life experiences have been scanned, carved, cut, shaved, diced, sheared, and sliced, so that only that which is palatable has a clear communication with a purpose. The shock or surprise isn't until you read section after section. It is then you will grasp the full understanding of "Standing Tall Through It All."

God, grandparents, family, and friends have been the cornerstones of my trials and tribulations. Thank you, God, for my blessings.

NEW AUTHOR

"STANDING TALL THROUGH IT ALL"

VOLUME III

By *Willie D. Kiser-Golden*

The writing of this poetry is about personal experiences from early childhood through life's journey of today. It is to help encourage, motivate, endure, and much more . . .

WHAT OTHER READERS HAVE SAID AFTER READING VOLUME I AND VOLUME II:

"It displays originally perspective and unique creativity. The poem, "Shout for Love" from volume I was awarded the Editor's Choice Award of the INTERNATIONAL LIBRARY OF POETRY."

"I was inspired to strive toward accomplishing my goal."
—Antoine H.

"The book is amazing and a great way to express feelings/ thoughts of things one has experienced and gone through."
—Viviana S.

"Many poems bring back memories of the old days."
—Susan B.

"After reading these poems, one begins to see strong love and how determination can make a person succeed."
—Dorothy Sikes

"I couldn't put the book down until all the poems were read. The poems sent me back down memory lane."
—Shellie Fitzpatrick, Jr.

Table of Contents

SPIRITUAL/INSPIRATION

GOD IS OUR DEFENSE

It is God who makes us strong
When things are going wrong

It is God who makes our pathways safe
It is God who guides us as we travel from place to place

It is God who makes us sure-footed as a deer
It is God who teaches us to have no fear

It is God who keep us safe on the mountain and in vallys
It is God who protects us in the alleys

It is God who is perfect in all of His work and deeds
It is God who helps us to succeed

It is God who trains us to battle obstacles
It is God who teaches us to use our strongest tackles

It is God who can make all things possible through prayer
so that we can be WINNERS

THE LORD HAS TOUCHED ME

He touched me to be helpful to others
No matter what race, creed, or color

He touched me to be cheerful and optimistic
Toward obstacles that confront me

He touched me to suppress bad vibes
So that I can live a bright and happy life

He touched me to be humble,
Keep the faith and hope I do not stumble

He touched me to do the best with my abilities
And sing a song with all the possibilities

The Lord has touched me with a finger of Love

BE HAPPY

Through my ventures in life
I shall have no fear
when the vision of my way is not clear

I shall strive to be worthy of Your blessings
When I don't know what to do
I shall not procrastinate my thanks to You

I shall let go of the past
And align myself with people who are empowered
with positive thoughts and ideas that last

I shall seek wisdom from the wise and the elderly
By being silent to their views
and remember their words to review

I thank Him with all sincerity
for love, security, prosperity
and for my HAPPINESS

I AM BLESSED

Born in the image of God
I am blessed and empowered with
His mercy
His faith
His grace
His strength
His trust
His word
His courage
His prosperity
His love
Through the edification of His teaching
I AM TRULY BLESSED

FOR THE LOVE OF JESUS
(BAPTISED)

The sun was sunny, hot and clear
I was not afraid, not an inkling of fear
I loved and wanted to be saved
And serve the Almighty Jesus

In the green pasture, there was a small pond
The water was clear and sometimes muddy
From the visit of black-and-white cows
God was there, He makes a way somehow

I took my vows and orders from the pastor
I believed they were words from the Master
My heart was pumping, and my faith was strong
Today I felt saved and reformed again by the Spirit of God

I was dressed in an all-white homemade gown
I was held by the pastor and assisted by a deacon
Surrounded by family and members in Christ
Everything seemed transparent

They lowered me in the water
Dipped me down three times
In the name of the Father,
Son and the Holy Ghost

I was wet and renewed in the spirit of love
And assured by God's grace and mercy
It was the day I was baptized, God's will had been done
And I knew in my heart, He would never leave me alone

THE BEAUTY OF LIFE

Our lost loved ones would not
have wanted us to mourn, but
rather to enjoy life and move on.
A leaf in life has fallen
in our minds and bodies we must be strong.

Let our memories light up the world
with love, joy, and happiness you shared.
Dress up and put on your best face of courage.
Wear a rose in your lapel or feather on your hat
and know in your heart that you really cared.

Cheer up and put a smile on your face
spare the tears and replace them with joy
nothing is or has been in vain
you are only here for full and complete gain
not to endure hardship and pain

Our beautiful memories shall always be cherished
in our hearts and never lost in the dust
God is with us and He is our savior
just between us, life is a plus
to know the beauty of life, love and in God we trust

Enjoy life and rejoice the memories
a leaf in life has fallen
in our minds and bodies we must be strong
sweet memories will be in our hearts forever
life is beautiful, so we must move on

Don't weep, don't cry, and don't mourn
pray and ask God to make and keep you strong
be thankful that she/he was a part of your life
celebrate the good and happy times you spent together.

Life is beautiful, we are not alone, therefore, we must move
on....
with love

HAVE FAITH
(Belief and trust in God)

With faith we are never alone. We realize that we have within us everything we need to overcome any of life's challenges.

Each and everyday we must pause to put on our spiritual armor. Through daily communion we develop a deep and personal relationship with God.

Ask for what you want. Let your mind scan life's menu. Make a decision knowing whatever you want is available. Ask for what you want, the way you want it. From that moment on, BELIEVE IT IS YOURS, THROUGH PRAYER.

The spirit within is there for us, always. We just have to acknowledge it, praise it, thank God for it, and know everything is all right now.

Remember the courage of our fore parents will give you the COURAGE to keep on believing and keeping on.

When you stand with the blessings of your mother and God, it matters not who stands against you.

God is as dependent on you as you are on HIM

There is magic in BELIEVING
When you are in love's embrace, all of God's blessings flow
toward you

God never leaves us alone. He is with you all the time. All
the time, God is with you on the mountains and in the valleys
HAVE FAITH AND TRUST HIM

I'VE GOT A TRUMP CARD
(GOD)

Life can be real rough, rocky and very hard
but we have the necessary
tools to sustain the trump card

We work, earn money to save a dollar bill
dream to cruise and admire deals of
the newest homes and cars on wheels

Let go the disappointments of the past
but never let go of your trump card
because it is one of our biggest rewards

Have faith, and maintain love and hope
always keep your trump card
it is one of your greatest awards

Don't be pushed around to be made over
even with luck and the charm of
a rabbit's foot and a four-leaf clover

Try to direct and follow your own mind
do the right thing and control your life
keep the trump card with you all the time

In my younger and senior days of life
I have experience joy and some pain in my heart
Now I truly know I have always had a trump card
GOD

REACHING OUT FROM THE INSIDE

In my mind and action
I am going to be helpful,
Cheerful, buoyant, and
Optimistic toward my
Sisters and brothers

I will not have a bad life
I will not send bad vibes
In my work, social activities
And in my moments of tranquility
I shall squelch negativity

I will interchange my ideas,
Actions, positive thoughts
And appropriate deeds
To encourage others
Especially my sisters and brothers

I will exercise quality,
Service and principles
With my sisters and brothers
I have faith that love will grow
And in time my love will flow

FROM THE INSIDE TO THE OUTSIDE

REACH OUT AND HELP THE CHILDREN

God delivers His assurance to the young and old
some are hungry, lonely, and cold

Helping each other is such an easy task
some children are too young and sick to ask

God will be so pleased to our giving
in return He will enhance our daily living

Reach out and help wherever you can
embrace the children all over the land

So much love and food we throw away
could help the children in so many ways

Children who have a hunger for our love and attention
let us help teach and guide them from penitentiary

The children are the future of tomorrow
let us help and pray for them today
and tomorrow we won't be sorry

HOLD ON TO THE ROPE OF HOPE

Sometimes your way may seem weary and dark
Friends may treat you from a long-handled spoon
Have faith a brighter day will be there very soon
Hold on to the rope of hope

Financial problems may be at its worst
The miracle from God may not come when you want it
But God is there and He will not forget
Just hold on to the rope of hope

Your health isn't as good or mobile as it used to be
Your mind isn't as sharp as yesterday
Your eyes are weaker for you to see
Hold on to the rope of hope

Limitations and expectations may
Seem short for moving forward
Just pick up a few grains of sand
Sift it through your hands and see God's rewards

When the rope begins to get smooth and slick
And you can't seem to get a grip
Put a knot in the rope and
Hold on to hope

When you feel stressed, suppressed
Oppressed and depressed
Don't give up
Just hold on to the rope of hope

As I grow older, I watch and notice what people do
and pay less attention to what people say
I pray for peace and love everyday
and to hold on to the rope of hope

HOME SWEET HOME

HOME
Where my spirit is lifted
my soul is soothed
my vision is near and
my mind is clear

HOME
It is my comfort zone
even if I am all alone
home is where the heart is
through blood, sweat, and tears

HOME
It is a place to examine your feeling
It is my congenial environment
It is my habitat
I like it like that

HOME
It is my castle of hopes and dreams
It maybe a mansion or a shack
It's where I long to be
When I want to be free

HOME
It is a place to make things happen
It can be a palace or a crib
It is a place where I can go
no matter how I feel

It is home sweet home

AMAZING AND INSPIRING
(I WAS THERE)

Oh, what a beautiful day in Selma, Alabama
It was a day that was celebrated and commemorated
for the Civil Rights Movement, in March, 2015
I witnessed it all, I was there.

It was over fifty years ago of struggle and efforts
that were put forth to have the right to vote.
Thousands of people came and went to Selma, Alabama
to honor and pay tribute and take notes

They were our fore-parents who were the foot stools
for expressing a right to vote and making a change.
It was amazing and inspiring to know
that they would not settle for anything less.

During the struggle of trying to have the right to vote
some people were killed, water hosed with force, bombed,
billy clubbed and bitten by dogs in order to stop the non-violent
protest of voting rights in Selma, and Montgomery, Alabama

President, Obama and family, NAACP, and SCLC were there,
to honor the people who lived and died for the cause.
Young, old, and people of all races and colors, were there
They all took part in the walk across the E. Pettus Bridge

It was amazing and inspiring to hear the songs that were
sung and the speeches that were made.
There were tears of joy, and a united
connection with people across the nation.

The march was strong and they did not hesitate
to press and continue to move forward.
We won't stop until the victory is won
One step at a time.

ANOTHER DAY OF DELIGHTS ON A SUNDAY AFTERNOON

A quiet, and tranquil Sunday afternoon
the entire earth seems to be at rest
a full shady tree and a freshly painted bench
life seems to be at its best

Another Day
The delights of friendship, joy and love
from associates, family and friends
just another day to make amends
before life's journey ends

Just Another Day
While strolling by the pond's edge
watching the fish swim by
Reflecting on the undisturbed water in the pond
are clouds, trees, and the beautiful blue sky

Another Day
Birds, crickets chirping, and frogs leaping
I hear and feel the unrest breeze that you won't believe
Blowing and whispering through the briar patch in the woods
a sound that's so pleasant you won't want to leave

Just Another Day
To realize the joy that life can be
Just another day to praise and thank God
for the support He has supplied and
the blessings He has given to me

Another Day
To be surrounded with love, and solitude
a place where I often come and retreat
It's here amongst God's creatures and handiwork
where peace and beauty meet

Just Another Day
Where all the troubles are forgotten
only the beauty of flowers, trees and
falling leaves beneath a beautiful sunny sky
I can feel the source of inner peace, and a wholesome of being free

Another Day of love

Keeping It Coming, Keep It going, Keep It Up

Keep the spirit of Christ in your heart
Keep the care and love showing

Keep the flow of prosperity moving
Keep an open heart for giving

Keep the faith of your worth
In your words and actions

Keep it coming, keep it going and keep it up

TEACHERS

Teachers are full of knowledge and wisdom
They are people who are always near
to ease our curiosity and everyday fears

We as students had notions of concern
we were ready and eager to learn
we had imaginations, ideas, and visions to burn

We had puzzled and doubtful minds
that were sometimes confused and not very clear
but, the thought of quitting school was a greater fear

The teacher's presence assured us in school
that they were dedicated and well educated
they were wise, strong, and very dear to us

We wanted to learn about old things, new things
and future things in school about adult life
They were teachers who eased our doubts about everything

They were our high school teachers who always supported
and understood our needs

MOTIVATIONAL

HAVE NO FEAR 2004 IS HERE

Slowly passing cars on the cold and icy streets
pleasant and familiar faces I see and greet
cars and trucks turned and rolled over
including transfer trucks and land rovers

Cars are wrecked, repaired and sold
especially when the weather is icy and cold
Following through on my dreams
a better tomorrow we are deemed

Back to college, where I am determined to finish
Many sacrifices and problems will diminish
Books are bought and written to read
about how to acquire knowledge and succeed

2003 I will see no more
only the memories of things and people I adore
My adorable aunt just called on 01-02-04
and a special friend is waiting at the door

What more could I ask for this year 2004

GET A JUMP-START ON LIFE

There are many paths in life from beginning to end
Be selective and choose a path of
peace and harmony amongst family and friends

Make sacrifices and bypass the things you want
and focus on the things you need
Develop a sense of respect for self and others

Stay in school or make a call to some kind of college
Enroll and empower yourself with knowledge and
Let your mind be captured by the rapture of well-being

Because we are worthy of the best things
that life can provide, by getting
a jump-start on life

BE A HIGHLY EFFECTIVE PERSON

Let your light shine and illuminate
The path that you walk and talk so freely
Define your purpose in life and
Spread the glory of your well-being for others to see

Be a champion in your own way
To make a difference day by day
For the good of mankind
Even when people turn and walk away

Let the light of your path shine through the darkest mask
And ease the tension of the heaviest task
Let every effort be a breakthrough as a witness to humanity
To be a highly effective person can help bring comfort to
families

STOP, LOOK, AND LISTEN TO OURSELVES

STOP
Take moment and stop, look, and listen
Look, listen, and stop

LOOK
Don't let forms that practice immoral sexual activities into
your world
Don't make it a habit to group or team up with people who
are always gossiping

LISTEN
Listen to your inner perception of thoughts and ideas
Get outside of our image and take a look at ourselves

STOP
Don't let yourself be surrounded or engulfed with rebellious
people
Don't get caught up in actions of quick-tempered people

LOOK
If you stay in a friendship with negative people you will
eventually
Compromise your ideas, thoughts, and wisdom on moral
standards

LISTEN
Don't be mislead by fools or frivolous friends
Don't put yourself in the company of self-indulgent people

To avoid these measures, just put your mind outside the box and think
Beyond the boundaries of a limited circle and STOP---
LOOK---LISTEN

THERE IS NOTHING LIKE POWER

LOVE is sweet
LOVE is kind
LOVE is strange and beneficial
LOVE is caring and understanding
LOVE is abstract
LOVE is power and endurance

ENDURANCE is challenging
ENDURANCE is bravery
ENDURANCE is patience
ENDURANCE is power and spiritual

SPIRITUAL is peace
SPIRITUAL is solitude
SPIRITUAL is sacred
SPIRITUAL is belief
SPIRITUAL is love and power

POWER is knowledge
POWER is strength
POWER is magnification
POWER is energy
POWER is authority
POWER is force
POWER is love, endurance, and spiritual

ACTIONS AND REACTIONS

Before I toss my chips down the drain
I will love, laugh, and weave out the art of failures in life

Before I turn and walk away from a problem
I will reach out and get involved to solve the issue

Before I deny myself the right tools to overcome obstacles
I will ask God to empower me with ideas to be practical

Before I am knocked down with frustration and defeat
I will dig my heels into the power of my determination of hope

Before I lie and waddle in my sorrow
I will get up and start all over with an inspiring thought

Before I turn my back on love, I will seek knowledge to
withstand
rejection and despair

Before I fold my wings and claim defeat, I will seek blessings
from God and claim victory

Before I let my actions and reactions get out of control, I will
search for the truth within to make a difference toward
mankind

Before I give up on trying, I will place my ideas and dreams
before a hungry crowd and take a chance on the loss

BE AN EAGLE NOT A CHICKEN

Don't limit yourself on what you can do
use the strength you have and soar like an eagle

Don't sell yourself short by what others may say
extend your wings and fly night and day

Get out your armor of guard and fly
soar the skies like a bird in the sky

Discern yourself with love and knowledge
be an advocate of the workforce or college

Branch out beyond the boundaries of goodwill
and glide into an upward flight with grace and skill

Be an eagle and explore the gifts and challenges of life
smile and sing a song of happiness and blithe

Penetrate the walls of silence and set yourself free
on what you desire or want to be

Don't let your mind become bordered by a fence
only you can make a difference

Be a personal testimony to unbelievers
and show them that you are an eagle not a chicken

HAVE COURAGE

Have courage to stand up for what is right or wrong
Have courage to stand up for what you believe in

Have courage to do something daring
Have courage to overcome worry

Have courage to speak freely the truth
Have courage to stand alone

Have courage to take charge of your life
If it means standing by yourself

I WON'T LET YOU RUFFLE MY FEATHERS

I will look you straight in the eyes
smile and walk away
No matter how rude you act or what you say
I won't let you ruffle my feathers

You can smack me around or knock me down
with a mind and character of a simple slob
I will love you like corn on a cob
I won't let you ruffle my feathers

Your disposition displays a lack of confidence
and a lack of respect to self and everyone else
it really doesn't make any sense, but it's okay
I won't let you ruffle my feathers

It is a decision that you made on your own
to create pain instead of love,
walk in fear and stand alone
I won't let you ruffle my feathers

I will forever love myself and other people
I shall smile and look them in the face
and gain respect from characters like you
because I won.t let you ruffle my feathers

ENDURANCE

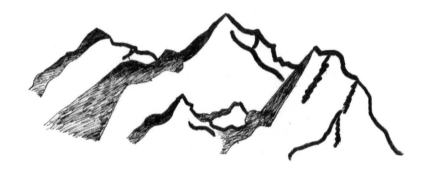

GOD, HEART, AND THE LAW

Sitting in a room full of magazines,
file cabinets, and non-working telephones
all of us speaking in a voice of different tones

We had visions and scenes of dragnet
we all would rather be at home playing with our pets
or planning a vacation on a super jet

Twelve frustrated jurors trying to make
a decision, in a cold room with people of the law
we wanted our decision to be lacked of flaws

One day, two days, three days
four days, we had to stay
for fifteen dollars a day in pay

It was a verdict we had to make
guilty or not on a crime so severe
in our hearts we wanted no mistakes

It was very hard for twelve diverse men
and women to act and agree on a verdict
that had so many loose ends as evidence

The evidence we heard made it very difficult
for us to become convinced on a
verdict with valid credits

We all depended on God, our hearts,
minds, the man we saw, and
the evidence we heard according to the law

THANK YOU JESUS, NOT GUILTY

WILLIE D. KISER-GOLDEN

WE PRAY FOR APPLE LINE STREET

Our hearts and souls are scorched
with problems and calamity
causing stress and discomfort to our families

We must make a change before it is too late.
The problems we have in this region,
some of us will never escape

We know what we would like,
for our neighborhood to be
full of love, unity, and a challenge to be free

Each day we pray for a safe
and better place to live
Our thanks to God for His mercy to forgive

Children should be taught
about love, faith and hope
not about hate, violence and dope

We want to see and welcome a beautiful
scenery, live happy and comfortable
instead, we hear gunshots shooting children deadly

We shall continue to pray for Apple Line street,
to keep the faith in God, and the people we meet
for crime to become a resting place under our feet

THE CHALLENGE

Skinny little children in the woods
Playing and walking through the rain
Forgetting just how far we came

A rising creek soon would be there
How will we cross over the water to get home?
There were no beepers or telephones

Limbs and leaves falling slowly from the trees
Only a small trail for us to follow
Until we came to the rising creek to cross

We were faced with decisions of hard bumps
None of us could really swim
And all of us were too small or too scared to jump

There were branches for us to seek
There were no ropes or twine for us to use
We were near tears and confused

Only a long, large log lying across the creek
We had but one choice to make
Walk a log, run a log, or slide on our bellies

TO GET ACROSS THE RISING CREEK

WILLIE D. KISER-GOLDEN

I FEEL ALL RIGHT NOW

I woke up this morning and looked outside
I felt some air, I saw the sky
I feel all right now

I thought about the good and I thought about the bad
I thought from whence I had come as a lad
I feel all right now

I don't have all that I want, and just some of my needs
I have done some wrong, I have accomplished some deeds
I feel all right now

I contemplate the future and what's in store for me
I have learned from experience that the worst will never be
I feel all right now

FOR SURE

The wind may blow and carry a leaf away
limbs may shake and the tree may sway

The branches may break
the wind is more than the tree can take

Some roots are stretched under and above the ground
some roots are flat and some are round

Growing strong, durable, and steadfast
deep and long for the roots to last

Looking at the trees helps me to know
just how much I can endure

For sure

WHEN A MAN IS DOWN

When a man is down, he looks all around
and it seems as though the world is against him
He goes his way both night and day and thinks
that his chances for getting up are very slim

Sometime his time is not his time
and reality is not what it should be
life will give him a friend
who will beckon him in and say not you but we

But first, the man must get up, take a stand,
live in this world and cease all of his crying
until he does, he will forever be
abiding a will of staying down and dying

A GLOOMY DAY/PESSIMIST

Sitting here all alone
wondering if I am on my own
a portion of my life has left
for me to try and find myself

I mope about my past sorrows
and grope of my unseen tomorrows
I know the world will pass me by
because it shuns those who will cry

My thoughts are negative night and day
not knowing some good, will come my way
I see other's good luck and hear their cheer
their source to me is just as near

The good for me I can-not see
I can't even say what will be---will be
I can't be an optimist with the bright side of life
Today I am a pessimist, existence is strife

I am having a gloomy day
nothing good seems to come my way
I will make it until the end, and the end will tell
that for a pessimist earth is hell

SNOW DEEP

Early in the morning shoveling the snow
Going from station to station and store to store
Trying to make ends meet and to make a little dough

Scrapping and heaving the snow near the fence
Before the snow becomes heavy and condensed
Only to a Michigander would this make any sense

Angel silhouettes, snowmen, and snowballs
Made and thrown by children and adults
Having fun and creating senseless insults

Cars on the streets driving easy and slow
Trying not to hit a post, a tree,
Or another car in front of me

People walking and hardly moving on the sidewalk
Wind so brisk, snow so deep, and ice so slick
No city trucks shoveling or spreading hard rock salt

Lots of snow lying on the ground
Not a taxi for hire or a bus in sight
Only a whistle of a little snowbird sound

Stalled cars and trucks on the side of the road
Were spinning and sliding off the streets into ditches
There were no pushes from Rams and heavy-duty Fords

Bumper-to-bumper vehicles moving very slow
A winter blizzard, the temperature was below zero
No helping hand hero or a truck for hire to tow

Snowflakes falling down, down, down
Ice on my car and front windshield
As I leave my job from the east side of town

MEET YOUR CHALLENGES OF LIFE WITH COURAGE

Investigate the odds and ends of your everyday living
keep the flow of energy touching all odds and ends
examine yourself with courage and understanding
and meet the challenges of life with a smile

Check out the odds and the differences of life
The most precious opportunities is life itself
Dig deep within your heart and soul
and locate the beautiful melodies of life

Search for the goodness of all patterns of life
with a creative conscious and an imaginative mind
Be the captain of your ship and meet
life challenges with love and courage combine

I DID NOT KNOW UNTIL

I did not know I was blind until
the calamity helped me to see
I did not know people until
I saw that people are not what they proposed to be

I did not know life until
living was strife and showed me what it was not
I did not know love until
the world showed me hate and for me not knowing I got

I did not know a friend until
one took me in after an enemy had cast me out
oh earth, am I or am I not? Please don't make me doubt,
for I will never know until

BROKEN NEIGHBORHOOD

Children playing in the streets
as I walk, glass and paper under my feet
no more cops walking the beat
in the rain, snow, or heat

Water from fire hydrants' constant leak
kids jumping and playing hide-and-go seek
weeds in the yard where homes used to be
replaced with dirt and pieces of debris

Houses boarded up and windows broken
young men selling drugs for a small token
dogs on large chains barking for freedom
someone call the news reporter or T.V. media to see them

Chalk and crayon marks on the side walk
adults screaming when they talk
dice playing in the streets
they are not the least discreet

Bar-be-cue cooking on the front porch
fire blazing like a mid-night torch
loud music from old fancy cars
as they cruise from the dingy neighborhood bars

The sound of shots for no reason at all
in your home a bullet may cause you to fall
cars jacked or propped up on three tires or less
let us pray for the neighborhood to be blessed

Now the neighborhood doesn't look very good
It's just a place called the hood

BLACKOUT 2003 (Detroit)

I can't study my homework in the text book
I can't even see how to cook
substitutes for electricity are flashlights, candle lights
and the sound of a loud motor generator

A yellow canary landed on my fence
blinking, at the many faces of people
something was wrong as if it sensed
there was proof of burden and suspense

Pitch black darkness surrounded the streets
our bodies were embraced with eighty-degree heat
the noise from cars and trucks were missing
only the sound of fire-crackers as I lay listening

Wondering if foul play was the cause
of the black-out 2003
or was it just a wakeup call
for you and me

Fruits and vegetables fulfilled the appetite
of hungry men, women and children
as they dined by candle-light
before they retired for the night

Running water was like a slow faucet leak
not enough to wash my hands and feet
The water pressure was so low
the reason why I did not know

For dinner I ate lots of lettuce
with two or three saltine crackers
and drank leftover room temperature tea
There was nothing more for me to eat

In my hand I held my keys
making sure all the doors were locked
In my home was a battery-running radio
and an antique clock going tick-tock

The next day, meats of several different kinds
were seasoned and marinated in sherry wine
prepared to cook on the outside grill
It was a reminder that this life survival is real

We never forgot our training
of basic common sense and skills
where there is a will, there is a way
We had compassion for each other yesterday and today

Neighbors sat on their porches before and after dark
friends and neighbors came visiting
and extending themselves to help one another
like a family of sisters and brothers

Before the end of the second day
of black-out 2003
the lights were on and running water too
We were grateful and happy, everyone thanked You.....God

LOVE

LIFE

The adventures of like is to learn and grow
The purpose of like is to grow and expand

The nature of life is to change or modify
The challenge of life is to overcome and conquer

The essence of life is to care and regard
The opportunity of like is to dare or challenge

The spice of life is to befriend or encourage
The beauty of life is to give or share

The joy of life is to show love and affection
Life is so wonderful if we just show love

CAN YOU FEEL IT?

I lay here in your arms
With a sense of peace and belonging
I can hear your heart beat so loud and strong

I can feel the pulse and sweat on your face
And the fullness of your body
In control of my body and mind

The touch of your feather-soft hands
On the most sensitive part of
My personal belonging

You kissed me and my mind drifted into the heavens
Your lips were soft, sweet, and warm
During the moments no other place I belonged

There was a love exchange in our hearts
So deep, so special and so right
We were happily married

DREAMS

My sweet and gentle love
I close my eyes and see your face
your soft lips I can feel and taste

In a soft voice I hear a whisper of sweet nothing
hold me close and hold me tight
squeeze me gentle with all your might

I can feel the rising of your pulse
nothing but the flow of blood between us
and two hearts full of dreams and lust

Standing in place you kissed my face
dreams of tomorrow and shadows of today
reflected our hopes and expectations of God's grace

COURTING

We had a slow, long walk in the park
listening to the sound of ding-dong
from a beautiful, large antique clock
as we watched the evening fade into darkness

We talked and stared at the birds in the trees
and noticed how fresh the air that we breathed
We held hands and pleasure we found
being together, when no one else was around

We talked about our wishes, wants and needs in life
the things we would compromise
and some things we would take a stand
There were more things we didn't understand

It was a way to get to know each other's
dreams, thoughts, and ideas
from one woman to one man flirting and
from one man to one woman courting

HE WANTED ME FOR MY BODY

He said he loved me no matter what
he often called and expressed his concerns
but all he wanted was my body

He called and told me love jokes
and because I could not relate
he said I was like old folks

He wanted to take care of me
he asked me to move in with him
and love him as he loved me

He wanted me to live in his home
to cherish love, money, and sex
I knew he only wanted to rock and roll my bones

Sex, love, and money was his fame
to me, it was his common game
there were too many questions he would not explain

I was wise to his potentials
I knew his love was not essential
because all he wanted was my body (sexually)

CROSSROADS

I am at the cross roads of choice
the choice I have to make
I need to hear your gentle voice
to tell me, which road should I take

Guild me oh Lord in the right direction
down this cross road of choice
light up the path with affection and protection
enable me with hope and victory

Lead me in the path of right thought
so that my route will flourish with sunshine
and my decision will not be hard to make
at the cross roads down the line

The choice I cannot make without your spirit
of courage and confidence
to marry this handsome man or
stay single as long as I can

IT'S A BEAUTIFUL DAY

In Detroit, at a beautiful, large west side park
On a bright, hot Saturday at a cowboy's bizarre
Everyone seemed happy as a country lark

I shall never forget the cold black mustache
That rested on his small upper lip
It sent my heart to a fast beat and a happy skip

I saw the glow in his eyes light up his face
When I looked at him in dismay
He continued to make his personal play

He stood there with a cigarette in his hand
With confidence, "I am the man"
As if he was the king of some sacred land

A raffle ticket I was trying to sell
For an organization dedicated to youth scholarship
The response of this man was friendship

He took the risk and purchased a ticket
Smiling, and trying to shield a mischievous glance
As if he knew, with me, there was a chance

His teeth were white that shined so bright
Maybe, I could get to know him and
Everything would be all right

Seeing the smile on his face and the glow in his eyes
I knew he wasn't shy
My heart knew, from that moment he was my guy

We exchanged telephone numbers
Never did I dream that he would call
I thought it was a flirt that's all

We made arrangements to be with each other
I invited him over to my home
I wasn't sure he would come

Over to my house, he came
We talked and laughed together
About life's daily trivial and the weather

Downtown we went to the annual festival on Labor Day
We strolled, watched the people, and listened to the music
It was a date that I shall cherish to this day

When we returned to my home
He brushed my lips with a kiss
I knew right away, he would be missed

I could imagine the closeness of his face
And the closeness of his body
· I could rejoice the sweetness of his taste

He left for his home state in Arkansas two days later
For me, it was a day of sorrow and dissipation
To him, I wanted to cater

From a distance we kept in touch
With phone calls and letters
I dreamed that our relationship would get better

Each time I talked to him from long distance
I could feel a passion of love in his voice
And a desire for love that was understood instantly

I wanted to be by his side
Love and desire is here with pride
I missed him so much until I cried

The kindness of his heart to me, he gives
Joy and happiness is how he makes me feel
Adds brighter days to the life I live

When we are together I hear music in the air
When he leaves me to return home to Arkansas
Life just doesn't seem fair

From his home he came to visit, driving a car or by airplane
In my doorway, there he stood
Each day I prayed that he would

It was like heaven was there on the scene
Smiling with faith that I was his lady
And he was the man of my dream

He is my king and I am his queen
When we are together, he is my sweet thing
To my heart, only comfort he brings

The destiny of our future is there for the taking
Our love for each other is there for the making
Neither one of us were faking

We were in love
ONE YEAR AND SIX MONTHS LATER WE WERE
MARRIED

THE MAGIC OF LOVE

LOVE matures you

LOVE is evidence

LOVE is confidence

LOVE is power

LOVE is synergy

LOVE is abstract

LOVE is giving

LOVE is receiving

LOVE is sharing

LOVE is obedient

LOVE extends productivity and spiritual growth

LOVE is all of the above and much, much more

YOU WERE FOR ME RIGHT FROM THE START

When I casted my eyes upon your face
and saw your natural masculine black mustache

I was mesmerized with your body
and magic of your character and smile

You were like the brightest ray of sunshine
as if you were meant for me when you were born

You were like a morning glow in July
I felt that all my wishes you would supply

You were like a warm gentle breeze in my heart
you were for me right from the start

LET'S GET PHYSICAL FOR THE MOMENT

If you will be mine, I will be yours
let's rub noes and touch our toes

Let's touch the souls of our bodies
and share the sensitive vibes of pleasure

We will smile, kiss our trembling lips
and grip the bareness of our hips

We will listen to the sound of our hearts beat
and let the passion of our emotions flow as a treat

Considering the time that we have been apart
there is a strong surge of feeling in our heart

Let's get physical for the moment

TRAVEL ME HOME WITH TNT LOVE

When I saw your smiling face
walking through the door of my place

It was a celebration of togetherness
a happiness that we shared

I kissed his face all over
he held me tighter and closer

I could feel the gentleness of his body
when he walked into my open arms

My sadness and loneliness dissipated
only love and happiness we anticipated

His presence assured me gladness
only brighter days of happiness

All the hurt and worries are left behind
we shall have peace, love, and to each other be kind

Now that you are with me today
I pray that you will want to stay

TO SHARE AND ENJOY THE TNT LOVE EXPLOSION!!

I SPENT VALUABLE TIME WITH ANOTHER WOMAN

When I saw her and she saw me
she was surprised and smiled into a burst of laughter
We hugged, kissed, and greeted each other

I was visiting in her town for three days
She invited me to her apartment
A familiar place, I had been before

We talked about old times, new plans, goals, and the future
The day was rapidly disappearing into the night
As I watched this woman's every move

It had been five long years since I had seen her
I wanted to make up for some of the time we had lost
Of getting to know her and she to know me

I invited her to my room, I was staying in a hotel
She accepted my invitation without hesitation
The hotel was not very far from her apartment

We walked, talked, admired the flowers
And listened to the Congo band playing in the lobby
Of the large, beautiful, friendly hotel

I introduced this special woman to some of my long-time friends
Who had heard of her, but never had they seen her before
This was a day of love, happiness and friendship galore.

As the evening disappeared into the night
We spent the night together laughing and talking each other
to sleep
We woke up the next morning laughing about the fun we had
yesterday

We showered, got dressed, and beautified
Ourselves before going to breakfast
And saying our good-byes

I admired, respected, and loved this woman
All the days of my life
Whether I was with or far away from her

The time we spent together was precious
Warm, valuable, and special
It was a day I shall cherish forever

SPENDING TIME WITH MY MOTHER

MY DEAR FRIEND SUSIE......HOW I REMEMBER HER

She was pleasant, smart and
a happy-go-lucky person
on her face she wore a smile
that was Susie's kind of style

When we were little girls going
to Hector elementary school,
holding on to the hands of older school mates
Everyday like it was our first prom date

I remember how studious she was in Math
and I cried because it was my weakness
but she always reached out to help me
to get the passing grade that I made

We laughed, dreamed, played and sometimes
we fought with each other
behind the backs, of our school-teachers,
adults and my grandmother

Yes, I remember how we fought every other day
walking home from school
fighting, to entertain a boy named jack
knocking a chip off our shoulders, to us, it meant to attack

We were young, innocent little girls
the very next day we were laughing, hugging and
holding hands, as friends usually do
and dreaming where and what will be our future plans

She spent nights with us on the hill where I lived
we went to bed with a flash-light on
under the cover, we were dressed in
gowns, that were made by my grandmother

We expressed the magic of our girly growth
we would talk about the boys, we thought
were very cute and sweet
especially, one in particular called Feet

I remember when we dated the same guy
we both thought we had it going on
the relationship didn't last very long
we were friends, and we knew it was wrong

Susie was always friendly and cheerful
even when I knew she was saddened with doubts of
dreams, loved ones, and friends
she suppressed her emotions with a smile to the bitter end

I never saw her sad or blue
only a beautiful smile with dimples on her face
always a touch of friendship and I love you
that made you feel special and full of grace

I remember the pecans she sent to me
all were freshly picked up, from her very own trees
and mailed to me, out of the shells and ready to eat
it was thoughtful of her, and such a tasty treat

I always, visited her, when I came back to Alabama
she made me feel welcome in her home
to spend the night and talk about old times
listen to music, and express what was on our minds

Only a true friend would be so kind
after all these years of being apart
we kept in touch through letters, phone calls and cards
our friendship sustained within our hearts

I will miss my friend Susie
but, I know that God has opened up the doors
to crown her as she enters His kingdom
to become one of His angels for-ever more

I love you, my friend

WE WERE BEST OF FRIENDS

We met at J.L. Hudson department store
over forty-five years ago
we introduced ourselves and
went to lunch together
We became friends from that moment on....

Although it's quite a subtle statement
well, it happen to be true
one of the best friends I have ever had
I am lucky and so glad to say was you

You were there if I needed you
and you never turned your back or walked away
I could always depend on you faithfully
anytime of the year, day or night

Some people have many friends
with whom they spend their time
but no one had a nicer, refined friend
who was as wonderful and special as mine

When your life's journey was over
I cried and bowed my head in sorrow and prayer
what a wonderful friend you were
I am thankful for the unforgettable memories of you

WE WERE BEST OF FRIENDS

ENTERTAINMENT

THE ANIMAL

I heard the noise from a room upstairs
I was alone and afraid to move
I wondered what could it really be
moving, sneaking and coming in on me

It was cracking nuts that it had stored
in a place it could not afford
to make his home where I peacefully lived
and not help to pay the bills

I tipped to see in short light steps
but I stopped and made a quick swirl
when I caught the action
of a brown, bushy-tailed squirrel

The critter was securing food for
breakfast, lunch and dinner
before the coming of the
cold, frosty, icy Winter

I could not rest the remaining of the night
until it had escaped out of sight
I would never sleep until it was gone,
out of my peaceful, comfort zone, called home

HOW SWEET IT IS

How sweet it is, to see your faces
After coming from many different places

How sweet it is, for your love and devotion
That makes me feel so happy with emotions

I am so happy until I don't know what to do
To be loved by so many of you

How sweet it is, to see my family and friends come together
as one
To celebrate my birthday and have lots of fun

How sweet it is, everyone paying attention to what's going on
Listening to music and singing a song

How sweet it is, to tell all the folks young and old everywhere
How great and marvelous the love we share

How sweet it is, you brighten up my day like warm sunshine
All of you are so beautiful and kind

My birthday is celebrated with family and friends
Shall be cherished and loved with my heart to the end

THE EYES

I casted my eyes upon his face
he smiled and said hello
I checked him out from head to toe
as if I had never seen a man before

He was so refreshing and real friendly
the eyes pierced into my soul
I couldn't hear any noise around me
for a moment, it was like a melt-down, I lost control

The beautiful, sexy, light eyes set my heart on fire
his eyes made my hands tremble
he looked straight through me and
my body slowly became pliable and nimble

His eyes captured my entire body
all I could do was stare, look and wonder
if I would ever see him again...
Yes, I did

COLORS

Color my cheeks an autumn	ORANGE
Color my hair silver	GRAY
Color my eyes and inspiring	BROWN
Color my nails frosty	PINK
Color my eye lashes soft	PURPLE
Color my lips vibrate	Black Cherry
Color my heart warm	RED
Color my eye lids sky	BLUE
Color my pocket rich	GREEN
Color my bills solid	BLACK
Color my smile a genuine	YELLOW

COLOR ME DIAMOND ALL OVER TO SEE COLORS AS
EQUAL

CASINO DOWNLOAD

Away to the casino to have some fun
where people go and people come

Taking a risk at one of life's biggest games
playing to win or lose is all the same

The machines you play are triple 7's, and Apple Jack
your money is gone and you can't get it back

If you are lucky enough to hit (triple 7's)
know when to smile, walk away, and quit

I cry inside, to see the money many people lose
but it is the fun in life they often choose

WILLIE D. KISER-GOLDEN

IT'S CHRISTMAS TIME

Beautiful lights shining bright
red, blue, green, and crystal white
hanging from the Christmas tree so free
a spirit of happiness is inside of me

Nativity scenes and reindeer statues
resting on neighbor's lawns
Children singing Christmas carols of joy
and wishing for their favorite toy

Mom dancing and prancing in the kitchen
cooking the family's favorite treats,
cakes, pies, and meats galore
a taste that cannot be bought from the store

Ornaments glittering on the Christmas tree
Dad shifting the log on the fire,
making sure the house is warm
when family and friends stop by

Dad's on a mission for the girls and boys,
putting together bikes and wrapping toys
The kitchen perfumed with a mist of fog
dad winking at Mom and sipping egg nog

Christmas carols playing on the radio
and the sound of Winter birds on the patio
Hugs and kisses under the mistletoe
when friends and family enter and exit out of the door

It's Christmas-time, a special time of the year
to celebrate and honor the birth of Christ with cheers
and to wish everyone a merry Christmas
and a prosperous happy New Year!!!

NO SHAME

Rosy cheeks and eyes blood shot
from all-night drinking and smoking pot

NO SHAME
Riding a bike up and down the streets
and sometimes talking and walking bare feet

NO SHAME
Showing no respect for her children or herself
and definitely no respect for anyone else

NO SHAME
A young woman who lacks self-confidence and control
will soon be lonely, gray, and old

NO SHAME
She plants no positive seed to harvest tomorrow
only a future of regrets and sorrow

NO SHAME
Talking to anyone who will listen to her plea
to make or steal a dollar from you and me

NO SHAME

IT'S A LOST GENERATION

A group of young boys and girls
Hollering and screaming up and down the streets
At passing cars and people they meet
No goals or purpose in their lives they dream
Their family is financially rich
But the children aren't worth a ----

Snorting and drinking and pumped-up hairdos
Wearing holey pants and name-brand shoes
Sleeping in cars with any man/woman in sight
All day and most of the night
It's a lost generation

A joint in one hand and a bottle in the other
Indicates a prime candidate for future trouble
Sleeping most of the day and partying all night
Provoking and starting alley fights
Is a nuisance to the working people in the neighborhood

Family members who can't see or understand
Their reason to holler and scream up and down the street
At passing cars and strangers they meet
They are young and out of control
Both of their grandparents are sick and old

No career, jobs, or study of books
Only the game to hustle by hook or crook
To make it through another day
Selling their bodies and joints for pay
It's a lost generation

Greasy and dirty head rags on their heads
Sleeping in children's clubhouse beds
That came off the streets from abandoned houses
That sheltered the needy of shoes and threads
It's a lost generation

Girls wearing revealing blouses and miniskirts
Boys wearing loose baggy, saggy pants
And double oversized white shirts
Their sneaker shoes are open and unlaced
It's a lost generation

Their grandparents show lots of love
Buying old and new sporty, fancy cars every year
To satisfy their grandchildren's wants and greed
For they too live in everyday fear
Of this lost generation

Their navels, ears, noses, and tongues are pierced
And a slave tether around their legs and on their shoes
They are rebellious and frivolous
I don't know what to say or do
It's a lost generation

Foul language coming from their mouths
Each and every word they say
Captivity of a lost generation will be with them
Until the day they die
Because they haven't been taught any other way
.

DIFFERENT STROKES, DIFFERENT FOLKS IN THE BIG CITY

Loose morals, no concern and less values in life
Nothing mutual between husband and wife

People roam the streets night and day
Will curse out before a kind word is said

Different strokes, different folks in the big city

You can go to people's homes, the first time you meet
They will offer you a drink of rum instead of something to eat

In the big city, mass production in the factory
Has changed the world to mass manufactory

How I wish I was back home where love is shared
With family and friends who really cared

MERRY CHRISTMAS

We have some things at Christmas
that we'd like to have all year round
like the wonders, excitements and
happy cheers of sights and sounds

We feel some things at Christmas
that we would welcome anytime
like happiness and closeness
that touches friends and family members

We do some things at Christmas
that aren't meant just for December
like reaching out to stay in touch with friends,
family and people we want to remember

Happy holidays with peace and love

KOOL KAT

He is not very large or a tall man
he is always sharp and clean
dressed in a suit or pressed blue jeans

He is a woman's man
He is a sharp kool kat

Sometimes he wears western boots & a bosalina hat
winking and flirting at all the ladies
He has never been a tall man nor is he fat

He is a woman's man
a sharp kool kat

He likes a woman with long beautiful hair
He talks hip just for fun
to the ladies, my name is John

Get the drift, he is a lady's man
a real kool kat

He drives a light blue, shiny Ford
He has been seen driving a metallic Cadillac
with custom wheels and pin-stripes

Occasionally, he takes a sip of whiskey or beer
with his family and close friends
and talks about the things that he loves so dear (women)

He is a woman's man
a real kool kat

He has not a lot of money, but he shares what he has
just enough to make the women glad
He tips his hat to the ladies, as a gentlemen not as a fad

He is just a very kool kat

Stepping, smiling, sporting, and styling in
clothes and shoes designed especially for him
made most of the ladies feel that he has dressed for them

Yesterday, and today, he still remains
a real sharp kool kat
My daddy, John E.

WHEN WHITES AND THE BLACKS GET TOGETHER

When whites and the blacks get together,
whites and blacks can watch each others backs
There won't be any race riots fighting and cussing
the people will cease arguing about school bussing

When whites and the blacks get together
there will be less complaints about
who is living in the neighborhood
people will be concerned about every man's good

When whites and the blacks get together
there will be more love and definitely less hate
The people of God will see that
the people of good will are going to celebrate

When whites and blacks get together
everyone and everything will be better
There won't be any tension about a long hot summer,
the people are going to realize that bigotry is a bummer

THE ELEGANCE OF A ROSE

A rose is a lovely and beautiful flower
It comes in a variety of colors
the stem is prickly, short and long
and the root grows deep and strong

The pebbles are gentle and soft
like the feel of a fashion velvet cloth
Water that rise deep from your water hose,
watch the rose grow large, and bloom so bold

When I touch and smell the fragrance of a rose
I will know immediately within an hour
how the elegance of a rose is extending
a source of power and glory to me.

CLASSY LADY

Classy lady who are you?
In that beautiful dress and fancy shoes
With your head high and body so straight
Walking with trophies of confidence and a strong will of faith.
Short, small and petite in stature
Well educated with a very sharp mind
Feisty claims the spotlight of this amazing woman
She is a powerhouse, trailblazer, and one of a kind.
This classy lady has armor against injustice
As a brave, tough crusader and has a love for peace,
And love for all people particularly her family.
The fight in her for injustice will never cease.
A cool personality that shines like silver
That makes her genuine and ready to speak and deliver
Words that express and motivate naturalism and modernism
While teaching young and old folk's classes on
professionalism.
Classy lady is a fruitful and knowledgeable person who is
admired,
Because of her teaching about life, social, and spiritual
experiences.
Many races of people and ethnic groups have been inspired
With her style, smile, self-dignity and aplomb
She is wise, friendly, and strong

Never does she yelp or scowl if she is wrong
It is her gift to help and manifest grace
To withstand the challenges of obstacles that one may face
A bright attitude like rich yellow gold
This indomitable woman has a diversified beauty for life
That can be canvased and viewed to reflect
Sessions of happiness and joy we can respect.
Classy lady depicts the beauty of life
That has empowered and portrayed the fibers
Of life with a lasting taste of sweetness and intellect
That I/we shall never forget.
NOW YOU KNOW CLASSY LADY (CORITA)

CAUGHT IN THE ESSENCE OF TIME

I came home from work on a Friday afternoon
In the month of October, early fall
Free from stress, copy talk, and hot air balloons
I took one aspirin and a nap to feel better
After opening up my junk mail and letters

A lot of rest I really needed
After a long day of hard work
I closed my eyes and was out like a light
For almost three hours I was fast asleep
Resting and dreaming through the night

I arose the next morning and took a shower
Pampered myself with dusting powder
Dressed myself in casual clothes
Picked up my purse and briefcase full of books
And viewed myself in the mirror to see how I looked

Off to work to meet the challenge
Filing paper goods and doing a timely work schedule
In the rain, I drove kind of slow
To work this Saturday morning I go
To do overtime for a little more dough

In my mind I wondered why people
Were going in and out of the bank
From the parking lot of Appleline and Joy Road
It was early Saturday morning and
This bank was usually closed

When I entered the lobby of my work place
The guard asked for my ID at the front desk
They only ask for your pass on the evening shift
Security informed me that it was Friday
It was time for the evening shift to work

I thought it was the next day
But it was the same day
FRIDAY, FRIDAY, FRIDAY
It never dawn on me that I had lost the essence of time
IT WAS STILL FRIDAY EVENING

WILLIE D. KISER-GOLDEN

GOING OUT TO MEET THE WHITE MAN'S MULE

Going out to meet the white man's mule today
is what I used to hear my grandparents say

And then they would keep his children, clean his house
and work in his fields by the sweat of their brows

They said there is a brighter day ahead, but to me it seemed
that at night they were too tired to cherish their dreams

Just a little hope was all my folks had
during the time I spent with them as a lad

Unjust wages and labor and not a union in sight
is really how we got, what they called ------night

Still they kept going and too often not complaining
sometimes they would come home early, when it was really
raining

They had it very hard sacrificing for me to stay in school
Just so I would not have to meet the white man's mule

So now I work in an office, they have central air keeping it cool
but the white man is still in charge, and everyday I meet his mule

THE BIRDS

Black birds, black birds, what a wonderful view
Flying back and forth to the electric wire line
Picking up seeds and worms from the ground
When my neighbor's cat is not around

Blue bird, blue bird you look so pretty
When you stand with your head so high
And the reflection of the sun shining on your back
As you fly away up into the sky

Yellow bird, yellow bird making a nest in the shrubbery
From paper straw and small twigs
Singing tweet, tweet so loud and clear
That sounds so sweet to my ear

Red bird, red bird how pleasing you look
Like a picture from a nature catalog book
Playing and making love to another with cheer
Reminds us that winter has ended and spring is here

Hummingbird, hummingbird so small and swift
A long, sharp bill you point into the blossom
Of the sweet-smelling honeysuckle vine
Bringing lovely, sweet memories to my mind

WE ARE CONNECTED

There are times when we don't give a damn
About ourselves or anyone else
Man, woman, good or bad
Weak, strong, right or wrong

We are connected

Rich, poor, old or young
Registered lawyer or a prominent doctor
Pediatrician or an electrician
Teacher or a preacher

We are connected

Maybe you are a computer whiz
Retired or still part of the workforce
A soldier of the armed force on a military leave
Or just a witty, comical person who likes to tease

We are connected

You may have a unique form of kindness
Real or fake personality
But through our pure fashion of blindness
We see the true form of reality

We are connected

Through success or failure
If we separate, participate, and celebrate
While making a gesture of affection
Or a point of rejection

We are connected

You may be a hard-working garbage collector
A farmer or a devoted housewife
Sending your children off to school
To learn their ABCs and golden rule

We are connected

There are some people who like to gamble
Some are well-known chefs who like to cook
We have fishermen who sail the deep blue sea
And old timers who like to talk about history books

It doesn't matter, because, we are connected

You may have a sense of rhetoric and logic
Or a heavy skill in technology or physiology
Speak the language of Spanish or Ebonics
Or a just a person who appears and disappears like magic

We are connected

Sometimes in life we are happy
And sometimes we are very sad
It is out of concern that we show love
To make each other feel glad

Why? Because we are connected

Whether we live next door to each other
Or far away from one another
A distance you cannot see
The spirit of love is the key

We are connected

We are connected by our beliefs, opinions, heritage, and values of humanity

WE ARE SUBJECT TO CONNECTION

A little something extra...

I WONDER WHY

I wonder why some people seek education to advance on
their jobs and others complain
I wonder why some people don't care about a rule until it is
broken and concerns them
I wonder why some people think that everything a thief does
is okay until the thief steals from them

I wonder why some people sometimes, lie to get attention
and get upset for their detention
I wonder why some people are friendly all the time and
others are friendly sometime
I wonder why some people are copy cats and never have an
original idea or vision
I wonder why some people work hard all the time and some
don't work hard anytime
I wonder why some people won't pay bills and blame the
system when their utilities are shut off
I wonder why I can see ten items and always choose the most
expensive one that I can't afford
I wonder why we do wrong and ask questions afterward
I wonder why some people start projects and never finish or
complete them
I wonder why some people wait until the last minute to do
something that is due the next day

I wonder why some people drive fancy cars and wear
expensive clothes and won't pay their rent
I wonder why some people treat their girlfriend's children
better than their own children
I wonder why some people judge people before getting to
know them
I wonder why some people don't know that harboring old
none running junk cars in a residential area
are destroying the neighborhood

I wonder why some people read and interpret information
the way it applies to their lives
I wonder why some people's minds are trapped in a closed
body instead of an open forum
I wonder why when you compliment some people on their
dress, instead of saying "thank you", they tell you where
they bought the dress

I wonder why some mothers support their children in their
wrong doings
I wonder why some people have no respect for time
I wonder why some neighborhood stores won't give a receipt
or put your bought items in a bag
I wonder why some people give you a fake smile instead of a
simple hello

I wonder why some people drive, cut in front of you on the
street and you get to the next light the same time they do
I wonder why some people are willing to give and others are
always taking
I wonder why some people bring cheap spirit to parties and
drink expensive liquor
I wonder why I am thinking of these whys (smile)

I wonder if it is because of human perceptions, skills,
techniques, and characteristics of human nature

CHANGES FROM BACK IN THE DAY

What happened to the games jumping jack rope and hill over
What happened to Sally going around the mulberry bush
What happened to the game hide-and-seek

What happened to squirrel candy in the yellow wrapper
What happened to Slow Poke, chocolate candy on a stick
What happened to Gingerbread Ike and Mike

What happened to penny loafers and black-and-white Ivy
League shoes
What happened to wide poodle skirts
What happened to baby high-top training shoes

What happened to metal spinning tops
What happened to toy pistols and rifles
What happened to two-wheeled bikes with wide seats

What happened to 78, 45, and LP records
What happened to the eight-track cassettes
What happened to the stereo that held, ejected, and played
ten or twelve records

What happened to adding arithmetic with pencil and paper
What happened to thank you, excuse me, and please
What happened to taking your hat off when entering a home

What happened to family sitting down at the table and eating together
What happened to ladies entering the door first when gentlemen opened
What happened to respect for self and each other

What happened to cars with changing gears on the steering wheel
What happened to cars with enter tools inside the tires
What happened to five-seat passenger cars instead of SUVs

TECHNOLOGY AND PROGRESS LEADS TO CHANGES

PHRASES BIG MOMMA USED TO SAY

Use Basic Common Sense

Haste make waste

Don't take the cart ahead of the horse

Don't cut off your nose to spike your face

Don't throw your body out with the bathwater

Sometime the longest way around is the safest way

You can take a horse to the water, but you can't make him drink

Don't burn the bridge you may have to cross it again

Take care of the little things and the rest will take care of itself

If you can't say anything nice, just don't say anything

It is better to have and not need than to need and not have

Stay calm and don't rock the boat

Every dog has his day and the puppy has the weekend

If I don't love you the pope isn't catholic

Don't count your biddies before your eggs are hatched

Some people don't believe a black cow gives white milk

Don't wait for your ship to come in, go out and meet it

Action speaks louder than words

A penny saved is a penny earned

Stay in school, because anyone can have horse sense

Don't throw a rock and hide your hand

Stay at home sometime, don't wear out your welcome

Birds of a feather flock together

Some people will steal sugar out of gingerbread

I don't trust him/her as far as I can spit

If he doesn't work or won't work nine out of ten he/she will
teal

If you do the crime, be willing to do the time

Blood is thicker than water

Treat them out of a long handle spoon

You treat me like a red headed step-child

Sometime it is best not to let your left hand know what your
right hand is doing

A bird in the hand is worth more than the bird in the bush